# MY NAME IS
# PEARL

JANIS BURNIE DESJARDINS

MY NAME IS PEARL
Copyright © 2025 by Janis Burnie Desjardins

Scripture taken from the New King James Version®. Copyright © 1982 by Thomas Nelson. Used by permission. All rights reserved. Scripture quotations marked (NIV) are taken from the Holy Bible, New International Version®, NIV®. Copyright © 1973, 1978, 1984, 2011 by Biblica, Inc.™ Used by permission of Zondervan. All rights reserved worldwide. www.zondervan.com The "NIV" and "New International Version" are trademarks registered in the United States Patent and Trademark Office by Biblica, Inc.™

ISBN: 978-1-4866-2643-4
eBook ISBN: 978-1-4866-2644-1

Word Alive Press
119 De Baets Street Winnipeg, MB  R2J 3R9
www.wordalivepress.ca

**WORD ALIVE**
—P R E S S—

Cataloguing in Publication information can be obtained from Library and Archives Canada.

# Introduction

God's love for us is unique. His love is infinite and cannot be measured. He is the Alpha and the Omega. He is the micro and the macro in our lives, surrounding us all the time.

> "I am the Alpha and the Omega," says the
> Lord God, "who is, and who was, and who
> is to come, the Almighty." (Revelation 1:8)

God's heartbeat rides the soundwaves and yet cares for the minutest details of the desires of our hearts. Our lives have much value to Him; shouldn't we value life as much? His grace abounds, shouldn't we forgive as much?

> Are not two sparrows sold for a penny? Yet not one of them will fall to the ground outside your Father's care. And even the very hairs of your head are all numbered. So don't be afraid; you are worth more than many sparrows. (Matthew 10:29-31, NIV)

The Father's love for us is all-encompassing. His love is priceless.

This story is one of strength, endurance, and the miraculous as we take a peek into the 101-year life of my grandmother Pearl. The focus is on the final hours of her passing.

# ONE

## Pearl's First Breath

*P*earl's story starts in 1914 when she took her first breath in a farmhouse in Manitoba. Born to my great-grand-parents, Samuel and Mary, they named her Pearl. The meaning of Pearl? As we read in Matthew 13:45–46, *"Again, the kingdom of heaven is like a merchant seeking beautiful pearls, who, when he had found one pearl of great price, went and sold all that he had and bought it."* This theme will develop a rhythm throughout Pearl's story.

Originally from Ontario, around 1883, Samuel and brothers ventured out to Saskatchewan and took up home-stead land in McCauley district near Welwyn. They were the first to break the sod in that area. After several crop failures, early frosts, and hearing that Manitoba was more suitable for mixed farming, the brothers abandoned their homesteads and moved their belongings, including their livestock, over several days as written by W. James Saunders in his research of the family history with Pearl and many others.

Samuel eventually went back to Ontario for a wife. On March 26, 1902 he married Mary Freeman Copp and took her back to Manitoba where he had built a fine house for his bride in the Pathhead-Beaver-Katrime district where his brothers had also settled. The local paper in Ontario mentioned that Samuel was one of the most prosperous farmers in Manitoba, having a splendid farm to which to take his bride. It also described Mary as a most estimable young lady who would be missed in church, musical, and social circles.

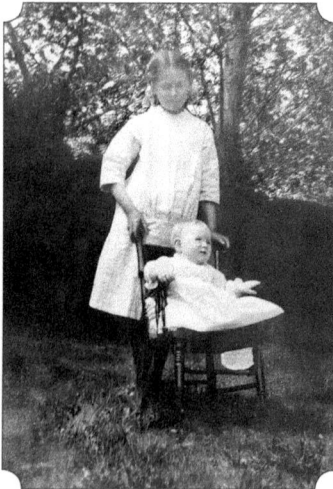

*Baby Pearl with older sister Iva.*

*1917, first professional photo shoot.*

Samuel and Mary had two girls—first Iva Lillian (Iva means "God is gracious") and then ten years later, Pearl Irene (Pearl as ref. beginning of Chapter 1; also beauty, purity and a touch of rarity"). I imagine it would have been difficult with no boys to help out on the farm, but the girls did their fair share.

The daughters revered their parents. Pearl always said that they were very kind, good, hard-working people. It seems their motto was "family first."

Pearl had many cousins. Her father, Samuel had ten siblings and her mother, Mary had eight, as shown in a family picture on the porch of the home which her father Wm. Copp built in Seaforth, Ontario in 1890.

*1920 Pearl 6 years old with cousin Kathleen in Seaforth, Ontario.*

*1930 Norman & special cousin Pearl, both 16 years wearing classic fedora hats.*

In 1920 the family moved to Seaforth to buy Mary's family home built by her father, only to find in 1924, they were called back to the Manitoba farm on business.

Of all Pearl's cousins, her favourite was Norman, who lived nearby. They seemed to have a lot in common, including an exquisite sense of style. They had fun with it and both wore classy fedora hats!

In Norman's obituary, the family gave Pearl an honourable mention, saying he was "survived by many cousins and special cousin Pearl."

Pearl and Norman's 1930 'classic photo' appears above.

The war separated friends and family, and Norman lived during this era. He made it to the rank of sergeant, then worked for the government, wrote short stories, and taught writing. His stories were read on CBC Radio.

Pearl must have been so proud of her cousin—and apparently he was known as Norman James (Jim) Little, something I had no idea about until now.

*1932 Pearl at 18 "Sitting on the Fence" at cousin Lizzie's place.*

*1934 Pearl at 20 "Feeding a pigeon" at Assiniboine Park, Winnipeg, MB*

*1932 Samuel, Mary and Pearl "on the home farm, Pearl, 18 years.*

## A Spring Marriage

Pearl married George in the spring of 1935. They worked on the family farm and lived across the road from her parents. Pearl then gave birth to Arnold, my father, at the end of 1935.

It wasn't a good marriage, the kind every young girl dreams about. She and her son had to deal with the demon of her husband's alcoholism. It was good that Samuel and Mary lived across the road albeit it would be hard on everybody but the good Lord provided shelter.

Three years later, in August 1938, sadly Pearl lost a baby daughter at birth. It was a home birth which her mother assisted and George attended. Pearl's mother, in shock, wouldn't let Pearl see the baby. The baby had suffered from hydrocephalus and died at birth. Afterward George took the baby away and Pearl couldn't later find the burial site, as he was inebriated at the time.

Later in life, Pearl told me that she had named the baby Narita Margaret. What trauma for Pearl and family!

In January 1942, Pearl and her family went through another tragedy when a military plane crashed near their land. There were several people on board and no survivors. It happened late in the evening on a winter night and in the middle of a winter storm.

As the story goes, when the plane encountered the snowstorm, the pilot tried to find someplace to land. But with the engines not working properly and a lack of fuel, the aircraft stalled and dove into the ground.

*"1935 Pearl's Wedding Day"*
*Pearl & sister Iva.*

*"1935 A Spring Marriage"*
*Pearl & George Burnie.*

*"1936 Arnold 6-month christening" George & Pearl*

*Pearl's Notes: On Dad's Farm, Back Row-Mother, Mrs. Shaw, Iva & Harold Shaw. Front row- Dad, Mr. Shaw, myself, George and Arnold on lap and the family dog.*

The locals rarely talked about the incident again. My dad never mentioned it and my mom didn't even know about it. At that time, my father would have been seven years old. I only knew about this upon opening a box of Pearl's pictures. There was a pic showing Pearl standing on top of a downed plane.

Pearl's family moved to Winnipeg along with Samuel and Mary, retiring from farm life. Sadly, Mary was ailing and passed away within a year.

Later my father made an attempt to fly off the roof of the family home's garage using a pair of homemade wings. He came through that ordeal with nothing worse than a dislocated elbow. I know boys will be boys, but I can't help but wonder whether he was working through the trauma of the plane crash.

Coincidentally, years later Pearl and my father Arnold ended up working in the airline industry.

Pearl's older sister Iva, who was married at the time to Harold, remained on their farm further south from where the rest of the family lived. She was a gentle soul, like Pearl. They worked hard on the farm and took in schoolteachers as boarders.

When I was a child, I only remember visiting my Aunt Iva a very few times, although I also remember hearing that Harold preferred not to have kids around.

Pearl and Iva always remained close. Pearl once told me that her sister had a difficult past, but she wouldn't elaborate. I'll never know if she was talking about a difficult childhood or something else. She wouldn't say.

When Harold passed away in 1964, Iva sold the farm and moved to a nearby seniors home. Iva had a little garden and was very happy. She loved flowers and visiting with old friends. Pearl visited her often.

Living at the seniors home was good for Iva. I'm sure living out on the farm had been lonely for her.

Interestingly, Harold hadn't believed in banks. When he passed on, nobody knew where he had kept his money. He was a very frugal man and farmed with aged equipment. He still brought in good crops, though, and implied that Iva would be well taken care of.

So where was the money? Could he have buried it? People did that back then, due to the depression. They didn't trust banks.

When Mary passed away, Pearl became estranged from George. He took off with another woman in the end. It hadn't been a good marriage at all.

Samuel moved out of the apartment and bought a small house, and Pearl looked after my father Arnold and her father Samuel until he too passed away in 1946.

Pearl's divorce was finalized in 1950. Divorces took very long in those days. Pearl became a working mom to support her son until marrying Andy in 1950.

She endured many tough times as a single mother. She would take any job, even hard labour. She worked on an assembly line moving drywall onto trains. I don't know how she did that. She was thin but strong, I'm sure. Employers didn't give their employees work boots back then, and I'm sure Pearl hadn't been able to afford to buy new ones. Despite it being a harsh winter, she forged on and wore her own snow boots, even though they weren't for the job.

Unfortunately, one day she slipped and fell. She couldn't work after her injury.

Worse yet, her supervisor brought her into the office one day and delivered bad news: "We aren't in a position to compensate you."

Those words slapped her in the face like a cruel, cold wind "Please reconsider," she said. "I have a child to take care of."

"You'll have to plead your case to the board then. It would be their decision."

She was given a date to address the board. When she walked into the boardroom, the men glared at her. After this inquisition, they refused to compensate her for her injury. The reason: she had fallen on purpose to benefit her and her child.

They didn't know Pearl. She was strong-willed and to the point.

They also didn't know what was coming their way. She stood her ground and turned the situation around to give them a tongue-lashing.

"If you think I would come before you and be humiliated, you all have another thing coming!"

With that, she left the room. Eventually she won her case and the board settled. Pearl was certainly a strong woman.

Having come from a background of churchgoers and missionaries, Pearl attended church regularly and was part of a few different denominations over the course of her lifetime. She kept herself busy and loyal to the church throughout the years, until she couldn't physically attend anymore.

Eventually she moved into an assistant living suite, but she remained active with her church, helping with baking, the ladies auxiliary bazaars, and visiting shut-ins. Oh, and I can't forget about her involvement with her favourite political events!

Pearl married her second husband, Andrew (Andy) Haas, in 1950 and stayed happily married until his passing in 1991.

They were avid bowlers and won a few trophies. They kept a fine display of them in their living room.

Andy worked for the railway, loved playing bingo, and often went down to the legion to play cards. Pearl and Andy took buses and walked everywhere. I don't believe they ever had a car. They preferred it that way. Andy also loved ribs, and Pearl made the best! He sure did smoke a lot, though, and Pearl had him smoke outside whenever she could, especially when the children were over. No way could anyone take away his cigs!

Still, he was a gentle giant. He enjoyed robins and they seemed to know they would be safe in his yard.

He had a stroke before his death. He collapsed at the head of their street, where a couple of teens found him and kindly took him to the hospital. He didn't live long after.

*"Pearl and Andy "in the wedding car, married in 1950.*

While at the hospital, the doctors noticed a wound on his head that he had been living with for years. They assessed it as an old wound from the war days.

Before Andy passed on, I remember that his behaviour was very different. He'd be bent over in his lawn chair, picking at tiny weeds and communicating less. I wonder if this war wound caused some behaviour changes.

Because Andy loved robins, I placed an imitation nest with blue eggs at his memorial.

Pearl was such a kind person. If anyone needed anything, she was there to help. She was a charitable giver as well. She had such a warm and caring heart for people and animals! She was famous for feeding the neighbourhood dog, also known as the neighbourhood mooch; we named her Suzie. This dog didn't live with Pearl, but she knew where to go for scraps! Suzie was such a sweet dog.

Pearl was also the greatest cook ever! I had dubbed her Mrs. Clean, too, as her place was spotless!

She included me in every activity, even with the adults. She didn't believe that children were to be seen and not heard. No one said such things on her watch!

Pearl loved gardening and I have fond memories of peeling peapods and gathering carrots for dinner, although I think I ate more than I put in the bowl. Even so, we were blessed with so much food that grew in Pearl's backyard, including potatoes, vegetables, and fruit. She had the farmer gene in her for sure, and I had the sweet gene in me.

I would raid Pearl's candy dish whenever she wasn't looking. My favourites were the tiny peppermint white candies with caramel in middle, as well as the chocolate peppermint squares. I would leave the sleeves in the box, hoping nobody would catch on. After sampling the garden and her candies, it's amazing I could still eat supper, but Pearl was a good cook!

On hot days, my brother and I would get to soak in the fishpond—without the fish, of course. It was a big stone pond! We also got to venture down the street to the real outdoor pool where all the neighbourhood kids gathered. But we had to be back by 5:00 p.m. sharp. That's when Andy had his dinner.

The airplanes flew so low over Pearl's backyard that we could see passengers through the windows. We would wave at them. It was funny to watch the adults talking; whenever a plane flew overhead, they'd stop… but then resume immediately after the plane passed, never missing a beat.

It seemed to me that my grandmother was misplaced, having been born in the wrong time and in the wrong generation. For example, she was very fashion-conscious. I suppose part of that came from living on the farm for so many years. She loved to throw off the farm clothes and get into fancy duds.

A picture she had professionally taken by a photographer in 1930 really captures in personality. She was wearing a fedora, a timeless symbol of confidence and sophistication. That's the image of her on the book's cover.

In her city life, she was fashionable and stylish, always keeping with the times. In fact, she was even ahead of the times. She was known to buy the *in* things as soon as they appeared on the market, from the latest TV to the first upright vacuum. That vacuum is an antique I still hold onto.

*Three Generations, Pearl, Arnold, Alice (my father and mother) and me.*
*Four years after marrying Andy, Pearl became a grandmother.*

*Four Generations, Pearl, Mary (Molly) Burnie (George's Mom),*
*Arnold and Janis 10 months.*

We never saw her with a bun in her hair. She went to hairdressers regularly and probably was one of the first women to wear pantsuits. She wasn't a little old lady in a rocking chair; she was more like an angel, sent to look after a little girl like me who needed to follow in someone's footsteps.

I loved sleeping over at her house, taking walks and talking with her. She was interesting! She had many long-time friends and was the life of any party.

One of my favourite memories had to do with the clock on the mantle of her fireplace. It was always ticking in a comfortable rhythm, creating a sense of peace. Pearl would periodically open the glass over the face of the clock and wind it up with a key to keep it ticking.

A homey feeling would permeate the house with a warmth that radiated from the living room like a mug of hot chocolate. That feeling made everything all right.

The clock now remains on a shelf above my own fireplace. Although I have no key to wind it up, the memory of its ticking permeates my living room too.

# Two

## Cherished Memories

I have so many cherished memories of Pearl. During my childhood, she worked at department stores, particularly in the shoe department. Her obsessive pet peeve was that her grandchildren have good, proper-fitting shoes. Times were tough for my parents, so I suppose getting employee discounts was a help, along with her special attention to shoe-sizing.

I had developed the nervous habit of walking with my big toes curled under, which created big indents inside my shoes. I still sometimes say, "Some bite nails, I curl toes."

When Pearl identified the problem with my shoes, her new career took flight.

Her other pet peeve was that she didn't like slouching. She was a gentle drill sergeant in leading us to adopt the

*Pearl, my Aunt Iva and myself "I was three years old in a brand new winter outfit and new boots!*

straight and tall walk. I suppose it was because of her own hunched back, which grew worse as she aged. When walking and talking with Pearl, our chats with her often ended the same way: "Straighten up. You don't want to look like your grandmother." She also gently reminded me not to curl my toes, or else I'd wreck my new shoes!

One of my fondest memories was the day Pearl arrived with new winter coats for us. She didn't just have one for me, but two. I was so excited! I loved them both.

But my bubble burst when she told me that I could pick the one I liked the best. I had thought I was getting both coats! Still, I felt very loved, cared for, and special.

Pearl also showed me so much consideration when she brought me to her church. She would give me a quarter to place in the offering plate so I wouldn't feel left out. She always introduced me to her friends, including me in everything. That was her personality. It's part of the legacy she got from her mother and in turn hoped to pass down to future generations. She believed that all children are special and created truly by the hand of God. That feeling of specialness was certainly impressed on my young mind.

> Before I formed you in the womb I knew you… (Jeremiah 1:5)

> For you created my inmost being; you knit me together in my mother's womb. I praise you because I am fearfully and wonderfully made; your works are wonderful, I know that full well. My frame was not hidden from you when I was made in the secret place, when I was woven together in the depths of the earth. (Psalm 139:13-15, NIV)

# Ｔ𝒽𝓇𝑒𝑒

## A Near-Death Experience

For I know the plans I have for you," declares the Lord, "plans to prosper you and not to harm you, plans to give you hope and a future. Then you will call on me and come and pray to me, and I will listen to you. You will seek me and find me when you seek me with all your heart. (Jeremiah 29: 11-13, NIV)

Several months before Pearl's passing, the Lord brought her back from a near-death experience. God's grace never ceases to amaze me. He knew that this experience would crescendo into what I will share about Pearl's passing several months later and His pure and perfect gift to her. God brings His witnesses together in His timing, as He did with us. This blows apart any theory that there is nothing after life but death. This shall be a truly powerful testimony of the love of God, who opened a door twice—first for those who were with Pearl in her near-death experience and then again several months later in her final hours.

These unforgettable events stirred things up. They have been shared not just by me and my family, but also by her roommate and attendants.

God is real and deserves respect. He doesn't live in a box, from which some may think they can pull Him out whenever they need Him. He is everywhere and sees everything and anyone. One cannot hide from Him, for He lives everywhere. His Spirit, the Holy Spirit, is all around us.

Best of all, we can have the greatest gift of all, a pure and perfect gift: the Kingdom within us.

> The fear of the Lord is the beginning of wisdom, and the knowledge of the Holy One is understanding. (Proverbs 9:10)

One day the phone rang. When I answered it, my daughter was in distress.

"Pearl is in the hospital because of a serious fall," she told me.

"No! Do they know what happened?"

My daughter elaborated. "She was found uncommunicative on the floor in her suite in the early morning hours. It's uncertain how long she had been there, overnight or just that morning, as she was found still in her housecoat."

I had a dream the night before and shared it with my daughter.

"Pearl was pleading for me to help her. I saw a bright light behind her. I believe it was the Lord. I also believe something happened to Pearl. She was in a panic state. Then I get your call and find out she's in the hospital."

Pearl had a private care worker who came in every morning to administer pills. Pearl insisted that she would keep her door unlocked, contrary to my concern that it would be unsafe.

When the worker entered that morning, she found Pearl unresponsive on the floor by the door. I told my daughter that I would check out the security camera data from the hallway.

And I did.

I followed up with the office manager. The camera showed the residence maintenance man pass Pearl's door twice placing his ear to her door each time which was suspicious enough for me but also the time stamp indicated 4 am. I asked what was he doing there so early? The manager said he was painting the next suite and the time stamp was wrong; and should have been an hour later; 5:00 am. A couple of hours later, the camera showed Pearl's care worker open the door, go inside, and rush next door where the maintenance man was working. Then emergency personnel arrived.

I still believe that the light in my dream was God's light, and He brought her back to us.

She never returned to the assisted living suite but stayed in the hospital until a bed became available in a nursing home.

Our heavenly Father loves us so much. He grieves with us and shares our pain.

> "Because he loves me," says the Lord, "I will
> rescue him; (Psalm 91:14a, NIV)

When the Lord brought Pearl back to us that day, it was a miracle. Praise be to God!

The doctor suggested I fly out as soon as possible. Pearl may not make it through the night. I booked the only flight left with a stopover in Saskatoon.

When I landed in Saskatoon, I took a seat in the corner of the waiting area, wanting to be alone as I wept.

That's when a lady appeared and sat near me. My first thought, I must admit, was this: *Why would anyone sit so close?*

No words were exchanged. She eventually left, but in retrospect I wonder if she had been sent by the Lord. I felt at peace after this experience.

I was only able to arrive in Winnipeg at 11:00 p.m. When I got to Pearl's bedside, my daughter was already there.

Before I could go over and give Pearl a hug, she looked at me and said firmly and directly, "You abandoned me!"

Both my daughter and I looked at each other in shock. Pearl knew about my dream! My daughter assured me that she hadn't told her it.

I then realized that it had been more than a dream. Pearl and I had both experienced it, even though we lived in different cities. But with God, all things are possible.

I was so sad knowing that Pearl probably had heard me tell God to take her. But then again, she also hadn't been able to hear me tell her to turn around.

"I was in an abandoned building and it was dark," Pearl explained, recounting the shared dream. "I called out to you so many times, but you wouldn't come and get me. And then you left me. You abandoned me!"

She was so upset with me that it was hard to bear.

"I would never abandon you, Pearl," I assured her. "It was out of my control."

My daughter tried to calm her. "My mom told me about her dream just this morning on the phone—and, yes, you were in it. But she kept telling you to turn around to see the light behind you. When you wouldn't do it, she left you in God's hands."

Pearl remained silent and seemed to have fallen into deep thought.

"I really do love you, Pearl," I said. "I didn't know what else I could do. I'm so happy you're back with us now."

Silently, I thanked the Lord for hearing my prayers. I also thanked Him for His grace in rescuing her.

Pearl didn't return to her suite after this but stayed in the hospital for a couple of months until a nursing home spot became available. While waiting, the Lord blessed her with a beautiful and kind woman to stay in the bed next to her. Her name was Marilyn. Marilyn treated Pearl like family and helped her the entire time she was there.

The two women ended up being assigned to different nursing homes, which was sad as they had become great friends while in the hospital.

# Four
## Reflections

Some time passed before the morning came when I received another crisis call, this time from Pearl herself. From her tone of voice, I could tell she was in a panic.

"Something is wrong," she kept saying, over and over. "Something is just not right…"

"Pearl, what's not, right?"

She couldn't articulate herself, so I tried to calm her down. I felt in the Spirit that something was seriously wrong. I hadn't heard her so incoherent before.

I assured her that I would call the front desk of the nursing home as soon as I hung up.

Immediately a call came through, this time from the nursing home. They had called me because I had power of attorney over my grandmother's affairs. They needed permission to send Pearl to the hospital via stretcher service.

I was thankful that my daughter lived nearby the hospital in Winnipeg and could meet Pearl there right away.

Meanwhile, I started the painful wait for a call from the emergency doctor. I didn't want to book a flight until I knew the prognosis.

Time seemed to stand still. I was anxious to hop on a plane, wanting so much to be there for Pearl as she had always been there for me.

I lifted the situation up to the Lord in prayer. I prayed that the flights would work out and I could be by her bedside and care for her needs as she had done for me.

> Blessed be the God and Father of our Lord
> Jesus Christ, the Father of mercies and God
> of all comfort, who comforts us in all our
> tribulation, that we may be able to comfort
> those who are in any trouble, with the com-
> fort with which we ourselves are comforted
> by God. (2 Corinthians 1:3–4)

Finally, my daughter called to give me an update. Pearl had a dangerously low blood count and there wasn't much the doctors could do for her. Apparently, Pearl had informed the doctors that she didn't want surgery and was okay with dying.

I must admit, I had a problem believing that.

The next call was from the emergency doctor. He suggested that if I was planning to come out to see her, it should be as soon as possible. She was bleeding internally and they weren't sure where it was coming from.

As soon as he said this, I flashed back to a vision a year prior when I saw Pearl's skeleton. Through the bones I was able to see that she was bleeding out from her lower right side and I awoke startled.

Had I received that vision for the present moment, in preparation for what was to come?

> And it shall come to pass in the last days, says God, that I will pour out of My Spirit on all flesh; your sons and your daughters shall prophesy, your young men shall see visions, your old men shall dream dreams. (Acts 2:17)

I asked the attending doctor several questions about what they *could* do. And what were the results of the tests they'd done? Deep down in my spirit, I felt they were holding something back. Something just didn't seem right about this.

> We are of God. He who knows God hears us; he who is not of God does not hear us. By this we know the spirit of truth and the spirit of error. (1 John 4:6)

I could tell I had put him on the spot. After asking the Lord to show me truth, by His grace truth came pouring out of the doctor's mouth, revealing his true colours. He became very curt. Because she was 101 years old, he wasn't prepared to operate. He doubted he would be able to find anyone willing to perform surgery on a 101-year-old. And if they weren't going to perform surgery, why would they put her through any invasive tests?

Obviously, this was not a good time to bring up the vision I'd had. So I came at the problem from a different angle.

"Years ago, I saw a sketch that her family doctor made on the back of a prescription pad," I said. "It was in Pearl's files after an operation she had in the 1980s. The sketch showed the spot where the doctors applied a clamp to prevent a blood clot. This is the same area of Pearl's constant pain now. Could this possibly relate to her problem? I could scan this sketch and send it over to you."

He wasn't interested in that. In fact, I felt he was writing her off because of her age. It didn't seem like anything could change his mind.

Our Father God values us. His Son is life itself.

But where was the value of life in this situation? It seemed like this doctor was just going to let her die without trying to save her life.

It was also strange that the doctor wouldn't call Pearl by name. He kept referring to her as "a 101-year-old." I forged on.

"Pearl may be 101 years old, but she has a name," I said, "She was getting along fine with her walker just a couple of months ago. I'd like to know what happened at the nursing home. Something must have happened."

Recently, Pearl had been placed in a wheelchair on account of some occasional weakness and dizziness. The nursing home had called me for permission to retire the walker and move her into a wheelchair. I'd have to trust that this nursing home was a safe place for my loved one and would make decisions in her own best interest.

When I eventually saw the wheelchair the nursing home had given her, I was shocked. She'd been struggling to operate this wheelchair, and I could see why. It was meant for someone with a much larger stature. In retrospect, this oversized wheelchair may have caused the stress on her body. It could be the reason that she landed in the hospital with a low blood count.

The doctor proceeded to ask why tests hadn't been done after her last hospitalization. This, too, shocked me. It turned out that she had been sent for tests a couple of months ago, only for her to return home emptyhanded since she hadn't been given the proper requisitions. The nursing home staff should have followed up with their resident doctor, but they never did.

The doctor at the nursing home did have a history of not answering my messages. And when I flew out, this doctor never made any attempt to meet me. I was always told the doctor was busy delivering babies.

Looking back, I can see that the nurses had a problem getting blood pressure readings from Pearl because she needed a smaller cuff than what they had.

The truth was coming out: the staff had ignored Pearl's needs.

At this point, I asked the emergency room doctor a pointed question: "What can you do for Pearl? I don't want to hear about what you can't do for her."

He explained that her blood pressure was so low that all he could do was give her a blood transfusion. But if she wasn't waiting for surgery, that would only prolong her suffering. And what would be the point of further tests, just to find out why she was dying?

Here I was fighting for Pearl's life and he kept sending me in a downward spiral of harsh words. He couldn't hear my silent tears over the phone, but they were pouring down my face.

Even if the doctor couldn't see these tears, my Father in heaven did. He heard my heart's cry. That's when I truly came to believe that the Lord was reaching down and holding my heart up with His sweet, sweet presence. The Lord gave me strength to disguise the sadness in my voice. Only heaven could hear the force of my silent cry.

> The Lord upholds all who fall, and raises up
> all who are bowed down. (Psalm 145:14).

> Blessed be the God and Father of our Lord
> Jesus Christ, the Father of mercies and God
> of all comfort, who comforts us in all our
> tribulation… (2 Corinthians 1:3–4)

"I need your decision now," the doctor said sharply. "Would you like her to stay in the hospital in palliative care or should she be transferred back to the nursing home for their care?"

At this point, I didn't trust him or the nursing home.

It was a tough decision, but I sent her back to the nursing home. At least I was getting a flight out to see her immediately. Going to the nursing home seemed less disruptive at least. I hoped it would be quieter there and she could find comfort surrounded by her belongings.

> Trust in the Lord with all your heart, and
> lean not on your own understanding; in all
> your ways acknowledge Him, and He shall
> direct your paths. (Proverbs 3:5–6)

I called my daughter, who was at the hospital.
"Is this a good time to talk to Pearl?" I asked.

She handed the phone over to Pearl and I made sure she understood that we were arranging flights to get out there as soon as possible. I explained that the doctor had told me that he wouldn't perform surgery.

Pearl's reaction shocked me. She was in sheer panic.

"No surgery, no surgery," she repeated over and over.

"You're not having surgery," I replied calmly. "You're going back to the nursing home, Pearl."

She was hearing-impaired and very upset, so I wasn't certain that she heard me. I wasn't sure whether she was upset over not having surgery or a misunderstanding that she *was* having surgery. The phone is not conducive to clear communication.

Anyway, I couldn't decipher Pearl's reaction over the phone and I had never heard her in such a state. She sounded so scared. It must have been a very scary time for her, having macular degeneration and being hearing-impaired.

My thoughts went back to Pearl's previous hospitalization, just before she entered the nursing home. We had been assigned a doctor and discussed her case. He had looked a lot like Dr. Oz and talked like him, too. I had wanted to ask him about the resemblance but instead resorted to talking to the nurse about it. She assured me that he got this a lot.

Later, during a consult between the two hospitalizations, I felt comfortable asking him whether he believed in visions. I proceeded to tell him about a vision I had about Pearl, since it seemed to correlate with the area where she was experiencing pain. I also told him that I believed in Jesus and took heed of such visions.

That's when he said a curious thing: "It really wasn't that long ago that Jesus walked this earth." He then wanted me to share with him the details of the vision.

"The vision showed Pearl's skeleton," I said. "Somehow I knew it was Pearl, and she was bleeding out on the right side."

He agreed to perform some tests, but those results turned out to be inconclusive.

Fast-forward to the present day. During the first hospitalization, Pearl had been one hundred years old and received so much attention from the doctors. Now, at 101, there was opposition to even doing tests. I was very upset. Was one hundred the cut-off service date? I wondered whether this was because of all the political buzz around the topic of euthanasia.

I still wanted a report from the nursing home but did not receive one. What had Pearl meant when she called and frantically told me, "Something happened, something happened"? To this day, I have many questions.

As for the vision, I truly believe that the Lord was preparing me for the future. Now I just had to figure out how to use this information.

I refused to give up. I called the hospital and tried to get in touch with the Dr. Oz lookalike we had consulted with before, the one who had taken the time to hear about my vision. Unfortunately, I was told he wasn't a regular doctor there and they couldn't put me in touch with him.

Next I called Pearl's family doctor, who had been seeing her for years. I introduced myself as Pearl's granddaughter and her power of attorney. I had attended a few appointments with her and hoped he would remember me. He did.

I explained the recent events, that Pearl had moved into a nursing home and was now in hospital. Then I asked whether he could assist, knowing her history. I also reminded him of the old sketch I had found in her files from the 80s, the one showing the spot where doctors had placed a clamp to avoid blood clotting.

> And whatever things you ask in prayer, believing, you will receive. (Matthew 21:22)

I offered to email a scan of this sketch and the doctor was kind enough to take a look. He indicated that it looked like the clamp had been placed in the area of a kidney. Because of her chronic pain, he wondered whether she had been suffering a slow bleed over a long period of time that was now becoming a fast bleed.

But he wasn't in a position to get directly involved. The nursing home's attending physician took precedence over him now that she was in the home's care. Frustrated, I shared that the attending physician at the nursing home had never made an effort to talk to me or even meet me despite continued requests.

At the end of the call, I thanked him for his time and quick response.

Interestingly, just weeks before this latest hospitalization we had been given word that Pearl had been moved up the waitlist of her favourite nursing home. She would be able to move there in a couple of months and get her own private room. She had been elated by this news!

Apparently her current nursing home had also heard the news, and perhaps this was part of the problem.

I called the hospital to inform them of this recent finding from Pearl's family doctor. To my dismay, I found out that they had already sent Pearl back to the nursing home for "comfort care," as they termed it.

Wow! That was fast.

In other words, she would be kept comfortable and eventually bleed out. I had to surrender the situation over to my loving Father in heaven and trust Him.

Under the circumstances, though, I had to question my decision to send Pearl back to the nursing home. But I realize now that if I hadn't done that, I wouldn't have the awesome testimony I witnessed at the time of Pearl's passing. But God has everything under control.

# Five
## Flight Delays

My husband and I faced unbelievable issues with getting to Pearl. The only available flight was departing on Friday at 9:30 p.m., so we booked it right away. However, a line of snowstorms across western Canada was causing delays. Snowstorms in September? Apparently, this has happened before, but it was rare.

My take on it is that the enemy was trying to prevent us from getting out to see Pearl. She was in comfort care at the nursing home, so we knew she could pass on anytime. We needed to be there and encourage her in the Lord.

Despite arriving on time at the airport in Calgary, our departure was delayed twice due to a snowstorm in Vancouver, where our plane was originating.

We ended up taking the earliest next flight available, which arrived at 9:30 a.m. the next morning in Winnipeg.

When we got there, we were exhausted and had managed a couple of hours of sleep. We went straight to the nursing home, figuring that the hotel check-in could wait.

On the way, we received word that my daughter's house had been sold. We knew this good news would cheer up Pearl. The house had been on the market for several months and everyone had started to wonder whether it would ever sell. It was a "conundrum," in Pearl's words. After all, the home was nicely renovated and located in a desirable neighbourhood.

This had been a huge worry on Pearl's mind, as she always worried about her family.

"My mind constantly twirls around thoughts and problems," she once told me. "I can't seem to stop them."

She and I had a strategy for those times when she experienced this.

"Remember what they say," I would tell her. "Ninety-nine percent of things we worry about never happen."

In reply, she would say "I know" and we would laugh in unison.

"You know what the Bible says about worry," I'd remind her.

"Yes."

"So don't do it!"

With that, we would both laugh in unison again.

I couldn't wait to tell her the good news about the house. It would be one less thing for her to worry about.

> Therefore do not worry about tomorrow, for tomorrow will worry about its own things. Sufficient for the day is its own trouble. (Matthew 6:34)

When we arrived at the nursing home, Pearl seemed better than I had expected. She was even alert enough to talk to us. This was an answer to prayer. I thanked the Lord for His mercy and grace.

My daughter mentioned to me that Pearl had been elated as soon as she'd been told we were arriving at breakfast time. Even though we weren't there at 9:00 a.m. as she had requested, she perked up when she saw us. The hour didn't seem to matter. I felt so thankful that we had decided to drive straight over from the airport.

We told her the good news right away.

"It sold?!" she exclaimed. Her bright countenance was a telltale sign that she had been relieved of a great burden. It really hadn't been her burden to bear, but she always took on her family's burdens—to her detriment.

I knew God's hand was in this. The good news was a great relief to the whole family, since my daughter and her husband had bought their new house before the old one was sold. But God had known that Pearl needed the mental relief of the sale before she passed. His grace and mercy abound. Mighty is He.

> Come to Me, all you who labor and are heavy laden, and I will give you rest. Take My yoke upon you and learn from Me, for I am gentle and lowly in heart, and you will find rest for your souls. For My yoke is easy and My burden is light." (Matthew 11:28–30)

We didn't visit long, since she tired easily. We left her to get some rest, but only after assuring her that we would be back after checking in at the hotel and getting some rest ourselves.

She seemed peaceful as we quietly left.

# Six

## At the Hotel

We checked into the hotel and flopped down on the bed, exhausted. By this time, though, I couldn't sleep well.

I read my Bible and prayed while my husband slept. I asked the Lord to help me through it all—to reveal the best approach in talking to Pearl with such limited time, to encourage her in the Lord and have meaningful heart-to-heart conversations, and to bring her back to good memories. And most of all, to anchor her in the goodness of God.

Pearl went to a mainstream church that believed heavily in works. She was big in volunteering and quite the worker. I often wondered how she could keep up. On one of my visits, I asked Pearl if I could record her story and she agreed. This is when I learned of the huge burden she had carried for many years concerning the death of her baby girl. She was traumatized from that event. Unanswered questions still plagued her.

I prayed with her, and I believe this was the moment she finally gave over that trauma to her Lord and Savior.

The salvation message doesn't mean we won't have trials and tribulations in our lives, but it does mean that the Lord Jesus takes our burdens upon Himself when we believe in Him. We just have to ask and receive as He comes to live in our hearts.

> For God so loved the world that He gave His only begotten Son, that whoever believes in Him should not perish but have everlasting life. For God did not send His Son into the world to condemn the world, but that the world through Him might be saved. (John 3:16–18)

Pearl had been brought up in the church since birth. She knew about the scriptures. It's just that she had been hit with a big-time trauma over the loss of her baby in 1938 and all the uncertainties around that.

I wondered if that was why she had kept herself so busy over the years, so she wouldn't have time to think about her past.

In fact, Pearl never talked about her faith. Ever since I was a young child, Pearl would say, "No politics or religion at the dinner table." She'd rather be silent than argue.

In writing this, it occurs to me that she probably started believing this way when she married Andy, who was agnostic. It had nothing to do with her own beliefs. She just avoided arguments over religion and politics while Andy was around.

While visiting her a few years earlier, she had opened up to me a bit. I could tell there were some very deep wounds in her life. When she started to bring them up, she'd quickly say something like "Oops! Bury the hatchet." This showed me that although her wounds may be buried, they could be dug up again. I can't judge her.

We had a good prayer time that day and I believe that healing took place. When we first say the sinner's prayer, we aren't promised not to have any trials and tribulations. But when we walk in His grace and mercy, giving Him all our worries and cares, we are renewed! Amen.

Many years ago, while taping her life story, she told me that she had something to tell—but she couldn't do it as long as my father was alive. Whatever it was, it must have been deep.

My dad passed away from cancer eleven years before Pearl, on the same month and day as her. Afterward, I asked Pearl about the secret she had been holding onto.

Looking downwards and avoiding eye contact, she told me that she didn't remember saying anything like that.

Perhaps this was one of her "Bury the hatchet" moments. She used that famous phrase whenever it was convenient, like putting a book up on a shelf and taking it down again.

I made some headway as far as understanding Pearl's go-to phrases. Perhaps that was her way of not dwelling on certain memories. There seems to be two sides to every story, though, and I'm in that learning curve. I look at all the angles of discernment and ask the Lord for understanding.

Pearl changed the subject to talk about her parents, describing them as good people who did many good works. I tried to explain that we don't gain entrance to eternity based solely on works, but rather on faith *and* works, which go hand in hand.

It's certainly a learning curve experience, but most conversations are about the interpretation of words—and then the clarification of words. The important thing is understanding.

It's been said that we all have to work out our salvation, but isn't that said for us all?

> For as the body without the spirit is dead, so faith without works is dead also. (James 2:26)

Pearl did come from a good family, as she said. They were a family of great works for God, which is what she had focused on throughout her life. They were also a family of missionaries, including Pearl's aunt. She had a blind uncle who did missionary work in India, weaving baskets and serving trays, treasures that I still have to this day.

Her aunt Ann Gordon, who died at the age of ninety-seven, was among the first women to pastor a congregation on the Canadian prairies. As reported in the *Winnipeg Free Press* on August 9, 1931, her maiden name was Ann Copp. She had been a lay preacher at the age of eighteen before immigrating to Canada. Women preachers in those early days were almost unheard of and her ministry attracted wide attendance.

In Pearl's lifetime, she attended church of different denominations with a wide range of doctrines.

I tried to steer her back toward thinking about her own salvation and continuing to work it out, living in Him, since only God knows what is in every individual heart. We must seek Him.

> But without faith it is impossible to please Him, for he who comes to God must believe that He is, and that He is a rewarder of those who diligently seek Him. (Hebrews 11:6)

Pearl had such a heart for people. She was the kindest and most generous person I've ever known. She loved her family and always thought about them. In the dictionary, under *worry*, Pearl's name surely had to be mentioned.

# SEVEN

## The Simple but Powerful Prayer

Before Pearl's passing, I often prayed the same simple but powerful prayer I had prayed for my dad before his passing eleven years prior. "Father in heaven, show Pearl what it would be like without You. And then show her what it would be like with You, in Christ Jesus's name, amen."

This prayer had a profound effect when it came to my dad, and I trusted the same would be true for Pearl.

> The prayer of a righteous person is powerful
> and effective. (James 5:16, NIV)

My dad was unable to talk at the end, but I knew he could hear me. The hearing, they say, is the last sense to go.

Like Pearl, my dad didn't talk about his faith. He never went to church, except perhaps as a boy with Pearl.

News of my dad's illness came to us very suddenly. He had thought his new dentures weren't fitting properly, but the denturist kept sending him home, encouraging him to bite down on them. Then he found out that the problem was actually caused by cancer. It was so sad to see him suffer. He passed away several months later at the age of sixty-nine.

Shortly before he passed, my mother and Pearl were leaving for a tea break. On the way out, my mother told me that Dad didn't want any talk of religion.

After she left, I said to my husband, "Well then, I shall pray in the spirit to the Lord."

It's always a safe place to pray in the spirit. Nobody can control what I pray to my heavenly Father. Nobody can control what I ask in Christ's name.

Some may think my prayer is a "patty cake prayer," but childlike prayers are effective! Jesus used few words, but those words were powerful! So why not us? He is the Teacher. After all, the Lord Jesus lives in our hearts just as He lives in the Father's heart. The enemy can't even think about going there. This is a secret place, a place of love and protection.

My dad was propped up in a chair. His head didn't move, nor did his eyes. Although his mouth was open, he was barely breathing.

I had such compassion for him at this moment. His mouth seemed so dry, so I took the tube full of water with a small sponge attached and gently wiped around his mouth and lips. It was the best I could do, the only tangible way to show my love. I know that if he could have smiled, he would have.

I sat on the edge of the bed and silently prayed for him, watching him closely.

Then it happened. Tears started flowing from his eyes and down his cheeks. My husband and I were in awe. We praised the Lord for this breakthrough!

My husband stepped up to the plate and went over to pray for my father. I reminded my husband that my mom could be back soon.

"She never told me not to pray," he said. Amen to that!

I silently prayed while my husband prayed out loud so my dad could hear. That's when I felt led to sing "Jesus Loves Me."

"She never told me not to sing," I said.

The nurse came in and took his vitals. She confirmed that he would probably pass very soon.

When Mom and Pearl came in the door, they went straight to his bedside, Mom on his right and Pearl on his left. We were all teary-eyed as Pearl said her last words to her son. To all of our amazement, he turned his head toward her and took his last breath.

Afterward I told Pearl that I had sung "Jesus Loves Me" right before they came in.

"That was the song I sang to him when he was young," she said.

I had no idea.

*"Pearl and Arnold. "1942 Pearl and her son Arnold, 7 years old."*

# EIGHT

## The Holy Spirit Nudge

After my husband's nap, we got ready to grab a quick lunch before returning to the hospital to see Pearl. I still hadn't slept a wink and was surprised that I was so awake.

We had booked our flights as a round trip and only planned to stay for a couple of days. We had intended to just say our final goodbyes to Pearl. Our initial flight delays had taken away one of those days we had planned to spend with her.

Now, with the newfound knowledge from the nursing home staff that she had been placed in comfort care and wouldn't live much longer, her passing was unpredictable.

We decided to fly home, according to our original tickets. It was the hardest decision to make. It meant that we only had time to see her one more time and say our final goodbyes. At least my daughter and family lived nearby and would be there for her.

After lunch, we joined my daughter at Pearl's bedside. She was laughing and joyous and so alert. It made our goodbyes so much easier. We hugged and kissed her. I thanked the Lord for all He had done for all of us.

The visit passed quickly and the time soon came for my husband and I to leave. We said goodbye knowing that this would probably be our last visit with her.

With that, we headed to the airport and handed in the keys to the rental car. The heavy air around us seemed to stand still as I fought back tears.

As we were about to enter the doors leading to the airport terminal, my husband suddenly stopped. I knew we were thinking the same thing. We made eye contact with each other.

"You should stay," he said.

Feeling the Holy Spirit's nudge to go back to Pearl, I rebooked my flight for another week, rented another car, and then saw my husband off. I rushed back to the nursing home and rejoined my daughter, who was still at my grandmother's bedside.

Cradling Pearl's hand, I whispered, "Pearl, I'm back. I'm staying longer."

She just nodded.

While I was gone, they had placed her on oxygen to assist her breathing. It was a grievous moment as I looked upon her frail body, knowing that she was giving up. Before leaving for the airport, I had fed Pearl a spoonful of pudding with sips of water. Now she wouldn't take anything.

The nurse privately told me they had no way of knowing how long it would be before she passes. They had seen one man prevail for three more months after he stopped eating. Pearl was very thin, so the nurse guessed that she might last a week or so.

Deep in my spirit, I felt this could be the day.

Now that I was staying, my daughter could go take care of her family for a while.

Since Pearl's roommate was at breakfast, I closed the door as much as I could to give us some privacy, at least as much as the nursing home allowed. Now we could have some alone time.

Pearl was tired and in and out of sleep. I was determined to give her my support by being with her in both her waking and sleeping moments. I wanted her to know she wasn't alone. I would pray for her while she slept.

# Nine
## The Visions

"I don't know how you did it from afar," Pearl said when she awoke. "Just wonderful! How did you pull that off? Just so beautiful! I just can't believe how it was raised up..."

Her laughter was infectious, but I had no idea what she was talking about.

"What was raised up?" I asked, laughing along with her.

It turned out she was thanking me for arranging a dining room table. "Oh, it was beautiful! God is so good. I'm so blessed! Such a party!"

I looked at my daughter and whispered, "She's talking about the table at the marriage supper of the Lamb. It has to be!"

> Then the angel said to me, "Write this: Blessed are those who are invited to the wedding supper of the Lamb!" And he added, "These are the true words of God." (Revelation 19:9)

My daughter shook her head. "It must be a wedding party or some memory from her past."

"No," I insisted. "She said that the table was raised up. And she pointed upwards."

Meanwhile, Pearl just kept looking upward in awe. She had macular degeneration of the eyes, but the Lord God had given her spiritual eyes. I truly felt she had been taken to a vision of the table at the marriage supper of the Lamb.

I thanked the Lord. This would remind Pearl of the awesomeness of the Lord. What a phenomenal answer to prayer! The Lord is so good.

Pearl's friend from the church soon came to visit and joined in with Pearl's excitement. She was still talking about the table and thanking everyone. In fact, she had a lot of excitement that afternoon.

My daughter and I went out for supper after Pearl settled down for a rest, and when we got back I sat next to her.

"What was that at the end of my bed, on the wall?" she asked.

I looked towards the wall. "There's nothing there but a calendar in a frame."

Because of her poor eyesight, I thought nothing about it at first. I just thought she may have seen a shadow or something.

But then she asked again. "Who was that person standing at the end of the bed?"

"Nobody's there." What was she talking about?

"Who's there?!" she demanded, becoming more insistent.

Again I looked at the wall. "It's just a calendar in a frame."

"Oh. Are you sure?" She paused for a moment. "Who's there…"

"There's nobody but us, Pearl."

I tried to reassure her that we were alone, but she wouldn't release her stare from that specific point on the wall.

I prayed silently: *Father, give her peace in Jesus's name…*

It would have been amazing for Pearl to be able to see something as far away as that wall. I pondered on this. Was it possible her senses could be enhanced at such a time as this?

This brought back to mind a day during her previous hospitalization. She had been lying in bed when she'd suddenly asked, "What's that? A plane?" We had all gone to the window. Sure enough, there was a small plane in the far distance. We could barely see or hear it, but somehow Pearl had noticed.

Maybe the same thing was happening now.

"Do you think she hears and sees in the spirit sometimes?" I whispered to my daughter.

After saying another prayer, Pearl was at peace. Curiously, she was petting something on her bed even though there was nothing there.

"What are you doing with your hand, Pearl?" I asked.

"Do you see the cat?"

"Where, Pearl?"

She laughed. "Right here on my bed."

At first I thought she must be teasing us, but she seemed very excited about this invisible cat on her bed. She kept lifting her arm and laughing as she tried to pet it, as though it was jumping around. She had the biggest smile on her face.

"He won't sit still!" she exclaimed.

Pearl had us all in stitches. It was hilarious and the room was full of joy. What an answer to prayer! The Lord is so good.

"What colour is the cat?" I asked.

"Black and white."

I remembered that Pearl had sometimes talked about her favourite cat back on the farm. It had been named Mickey, and in fact I had a picture of Mickey in a rattan laundry basket at home.

"Is it Mickey?" I wondered aloud.

She fell silent and didn't answer. The question seemed to upset her, so I changed the subject immediately.

In the past, she had told me that Mickey and their farm dog had met their demise at the hands of her first husband when moving from the farm to Winnipeg. In retrospect, I believe she was given a vision of Mickey in good times. I was saddened that I may have brought up a memory of bad times.

Pearl seemed to be very tired now, so we left the room.

# TEN

## The Three

The following account was witnessed in part with my daughter, some nurses, and Pearl's roommate. One of the nurses asked permission to listen and take notes during this sacred experience, confirming what happened. This nurse was fascinated by what she saw, as she had never witnessed anything like it before.

This is truly a story of the goodness of God.

When I returned to Pearl's hospital room, her attention was still focused on the wall at the end of her bed. Her eyes were fixed on the same spot, right around where the framed calendar was hung. Then her eyes moved above the calendar to a spot nearer the ceiling.

"Yes," she said.

I realized that she was conversing with someone. Her eyes were moving back and forth between three different positions.

"Who are you talking to?" I asked her.

"The Three."

"Who are the Three?"

She didn't answer. She seemed intent on listening to whatever they were saying to her. Perhaps she couldn't even hear me.

My daughter motioned for me to stop talking to her.

The revelation sank in that we were being allowed this privilege to see one side of a truly deep spiritual conversation. Pearl didn't seem to be confined to her disabilities anymore; she seemed to see and hear perfectly well, but only to the Three.

I believe the Three refers to Father God, His Son, and the Holy Spirit.

God opens and closes doors in the spiritual realm, and perhaps Pearl was going through a reckoning. One of her responses during this spiritual encounter, spoken in a low and solemn voice, was "That was a long time ago," After that, there was a long pause.

Those who believe in the death and resurrection of Christ Jesus also accept that He bore our sins once and for all. With a repentant heart, we are forgiven. We've been paid for at a great price and it is forever.

Pearl believed in God and knew that Jesus was God's Son. She also believed in living a good life.

I believe we have to tread very carefully on this and be careful of our judgments.

Now was her time. I trust that this story will speak volumes to everyone who reads and shares it.

I believe everyone will face an ultimate reckoning. That's why it is so important to live every day with a repentant heart. That's where the Lord, our Savior Christ Jesus, comes in. We must allow Him to live in us so we are washed by His sacrificial blood, sanctifying us past, present, and future. We need to be ready.

By the grace of God, those of us in the hospital room that day were allowed to hear her responses as she went through this reckoning. From her side of the conversation, it seemed like she was recounting her past. We heard her say many things.

"That's awful. I feel terrible. I should have said something. If I had known, I wouldn't have said that. I'm so sorry that happened."

She also answered "Yes" many times in a low tone.

Pearl mentioned twins, as well as a four-year-old girl with whom she wanted to take a picture before she passed on.

"I don't want to go to hell," she even said at one point. "I don't know much about heaven but would like to know more."

I asked her if she saw anyone she knew. She didn't respond to this at first.

"Do you see your dad?" I asked.

"No."

"Your mom?"

"Yes."

"Your son?"

"No."

Then there was a short pause. It seemed like she was listening to the Three speak to her again.

Then she said, "There will be more."

Pearl's roommate came into the room and overheard some of the answers Pearl gave in her conversation with the Three. This woman turned to me and asked how long Pearl had been talking to the Divine. This roommate was Mennonite and recognized what was going on.

"It's been going on since suppertime," I explained.

Nothing seemed to disturb my grandmother as she talked to the Three. The encounter was intense. Her eyes moved back and forth between the three positions on the wall as they seemed to ask her questions in an orderly fashion.

Nurses peeked in periodically, asking about whether Pearl needed meds for pain, a turnover in bed, or change of nightgown. I just told them that she hasn't asked or complained of anything and I didn't want to disturb her right now.

One nurse came in and checked the colouring of her legs. His shift was about to end, but he was kind enough to ask whether I wanted a cot set up next to Pearl's bedside so I could sleep over. According to him, she would probably pass that very night.

I thanked him for the offer and he set up the cot.

Apparently Pearl was the main topic of conversation among the nurses on the evening shift.

"Who is she talking to?" one nurse sheepishly whispered.

"She's talking to the Three, as she calls them," I said. "I can only hear her answers. It's a one-sided conversation. By her answers, I'd say she's going through a reckoning of her whole life…"

I felt so privileged and blessed that God gave me this chance to glimpse into Pearl's encounter with Him. We were all in awe.

"What is your faith?" I asked the nurse.

"Baptist. But I've never seen anything like this before."

She was so fascinated and asked if she could come back during her break so she could listen in. I agreed to this.

Since Pearl seemed to be doing okay, I went out to take another break.

# ELEVEN

## The Pure & Perfect Gift of Jesus

When I arrived back, the nurse called me over to the nurses' station to explain what had happened to Pearl after I had left. She had become very restless and kept trying to take off her oxygen mask.

Sure enough, when I went into her room the oxygen mask was off and resting under her chin. The nurse put it back on.

Later on, the thought came to me that the oxygen mask was hindering conversing with the Three. That might have been why she took it off and placed it on her chin when they left.

I stayed by Pearl's bedside with my daughter. Pearl was in a state of panic and confusion.

"Take me home, to the airport," she was saying. "I have to catch the delivery man."

As I held her hand, I called her name softly.

"Pearl."

She looked startled, realized I was back, and stopped panicking. I told her who I was just in case she was confused. I reassured her that she was still there at the nursing home with me and didn't need to worry.

"What happened when I was away?" I calmly asked.

"The delivery man had a package for me. No, two packages. I didn't know what to do. He left before I could accept them. I guess I took too long."

She wanted me to take her to the airport so she could catch up with this man. She was so distraught and confused.

"If it's important, he will be back," I told her. "And if he comes back, just tell him that you want the pure and perfect gift of Jesus."

This just rolled off my tongue. It must have come from the Lord, as I had never used that phrase before.

She calmed right down, turned her head to me for the first time in hours, and locked her eyes on me. "Is that all?"

"Yes, that's all," I said.

This definitely had to have come from the Lord, because she immediately felt at peace and drifted off to sleep.

I found it interesting that this was the second time I'd heard a dying person refer to needing to get to the airport, and in both cases it was spoken in sheer panic. During her first near-death experience, a priest sharing a room with Pearl had mentioned his need to go to the airport. Even today, I continue to ponder this.

I watched Pearl sleep peacefully. The Lord is so good!

Many months later, while reading more about the fruit of the Spirit and the goodness of God, I fell upon this verse in James 1:17: *"Every good gift and every perfect gift is from above, and comes down from the Father of lights, with whom there is no variation or shadow of turning"* (James 1:17).

My daughter and her daughter arrived at 11:00 p.m. I was so glad she arrived with her mom. Our plan had been to take a picture together. I didn't want to startle Pearl, so I just took her hand and told her that we were laying hands on her right arm to take a picture, representing the generations of our family. Only one generation (her son) was missing, since he had passed before her.

To this day, that is a legacy picture.

It was very hard on all of us knowing that she would be passing very soon. She was breathing slowly now with the assistance of oxygen. We knew it wouldn't be long.

Around midnight, we heard a senior across the hall yelling.

"Where did you come from? You don't belong here!"

Then there was another voice.

"No one is here! Go back to sleep."

Because of this, I drew my chair up next to Pearl and watched her chest. A nurse had already shut the door so we could have some quiet, due to the unrest across the hall.

I watched the slightest movements of her breathing…
until I could see no more. She lay there so peacefully.

My tears flowed and I couldn't stop them. There are tears
even as I write this.

Then I spoke my last words to her: "I love you, Pearl."

I'm so grateful that her passing was quiet and peaceful.

Midnight had come and gone and it was a new day. It
later struck me that Pearl passed on the same day and month
as her son, my father. For some uncanny reason, I wonder
about this. By holding her last breath until after midnight,
she and her son shared the same day and month of passing.

*Pearl's note on back: From L-R Jim Briscoe (Aunt Ellen), Uncle Walter, Dad, Mother, Grandpa Little – March 28, 1902 "Marriage of Samuel Little and Mary Freeman Copp".*

*100th invitation 2014 'Forever Young' Pearl's 100th Birthday with her great great grandchildren.*

# Twelve

## An Amazing Journey

The love of God is so expansive. He cares even in the minutest details of the desires of your heart. By His grace, He heard my prayer for Pearl.

There is no doubt in my mind that He showed her what she needed to see and told her what she needed to hear. After all, we heard her say, "I don't want to go to hell… I don't know much about heaven but would like to know more."

He has everything under control. Amen! What a gift He gave to me.

> If you then, being evil, know how to give good gifts to your children, how much more will your Father who is in heaven give good things to those who ask Him! (Matthew 7:11)

I believe that the Lord showed me the degree to which Pearl always second-guessed herself and never asked questions. But it dawned on me that maybe no one asked her if she had any questions about her faith. I didn't—that is, until that important heart-to-heart conversation I had with her.

Even to the end, we weren't quite sure where she stood in her faith, but she believed in God but would proclaim Jesus to be God's Son.

The Lord has lifted my heart throughout the story. It's been a tremendous journey of faith and my hope is that this story will be a blessing to everyone who reads it.

> And whatever things you ask in prayer, believing, you will receive. (Matthew 21:22)

In sharing this story, I believe that the Lord has been showing me to *simplify*. Everyone receives differently, as we are all unique individuals. Some understand by pictures and others by words.

Though I've simplified the story, however, I have not watered it down, something which Jesus taught us. When witnessing, we walk in the Spirit. The Holy Spirit leads us and continues to work with us.

The Holy Spirit was drawing Pearl to God right up to her passing. This is the goodness of God.

As Jesus said,

No one can come to Me unless the Father who sent Me draws him; and I will raise him up at the last day. It is written in the prophets, "And they shall all be taught by God." Therefore everyone who has heard and learned from the Father comes to Me. Not that anyone has seen the Father, except He who is from God; He has seen the Father. Most assuredly, I say to you, he who believes in Me has everlasting life. I am the bread of life. Your fathers ate the manna in the wilderness, and are dead. This is the bread which comes down from heaven, that one may eat of it and not die. I am the living bread which came down from heaven. If anyone eats of this bread, he will live forever; and the bread that I shall give is My flesh, which I shall give for the life of the world…

Most assuredly, I say to you, unless you eat the flesh of the Son of Man and drink His blood, you have no life in you. Whoever eats My flesh and drinks My blood has eternal life, and I will raise him up at the last day. For My flesh is food indeed, and My blood is drink indeed. He who eats My flesh and drinks My blood abides in Me, and I in him. As the living Father sent Me, and I

live because of the Father, so he who feeds
on Me will live because of Me. This is the
bread which came down from heaven—not
as your fathers ate the manna, and are dead.
He who eats this bread will live forever.
(John 6:44–51, 53–58)

Jesus also clarified, *"It is the Spirit who gives life; the flesh
profits nothing. The words that I speak to you are spirit, and they
are life"* (John 6:63).

He spoke many other parables to reach us at our own level of understanding. He used few words to get things done, whether it was to perform a healing or cast out demons.

This is why asking for the pure and perfect gift of Jesus spoke volumes to Pearl. It is simple. That's why Pearl replied by asking, "Is that all?"

While it is important to simplify, it is also important to *clarify*. Especially for the elderly, a lot of talk can be hard to process. And Pearl's disabilities must have made it even harder.

The Lord never leaves us or forsakes us. Amen to that!

I believe the Lord simplified things for Pearl. The instruction to ask for the pure and perfect gift of Jesus was profound to her. In that moment, I believe she finally got it.

At that day you will know that I am in My
Father, and you in Me, and I in you. (John
14:20)

What happened after Pearl's reckoning with the Three? Only God knows. As for me, what an amazing journey it was just to be with Pearl at this critical time.

Pearl loved life. She always talked about turning one hundred, like a relative who lived until one hundred and ten days who also believed in reaching that same milestone.

When she turned 101, I still encouraged her to keep enjoying life. I would remind her that it was only a couple of months before she could move to her favourite nursing home, or only a few months until her birthday bash at 102.

"Oh, I think my expiry date is up," she would say, jokingly waving me off.

She also never lost her sense of humour. I loved that about Pearl. She was always the life of any party. I surely miss her. She wasn't just my grandmother; she was my friend.

I miss my conversations with her. I miss ending the day with her, having a bowl of cereal or toast before bedtime. Before I'd fly back after a visit, it would be so hard to say goodbye. Living so far away was challenging.

After her passing, a couple of people approached me to say, "You know she didn't want to live to 102." And I was her power of attorney! Why would they feel the need to tell me this? Pearl never said anything like that to me. It made me wonder whether other people had been trying to convince her of that. Why would they do such a thing? At the time of her passing, she had been so excited to move into a new nursing home.

But something happened that day when she called me in a panic. Those were the words that started her final decline.

And I never found out what happened.

During the previous hospitalization, after her bad fall, I stayed by Pearl's side. She was in great pain. An elderly priest in the same room as her had also been in great pain. He exclaimed, "Let me die." Then Pearl also exclaimed, "Let me die." But this was the pain talking, I'm sure. I believe the same was true for the priest.

Pearl left a family to be proud of. At the time of her passing she had three grandchildren (including myself); one great-grandchild, three great-great-grandchildren with another shortly after and two great-great-great-grandchildren to date and growing. Family was her treasure! As the Bible says, *"For where your treasure is, there your heart will be also"* (Matthew 6:21, Luke 12:34). How much more family in Christ will we have in heaven? It's phenomenal!

Jesus used few words to get things done, and He performed miracles for believing and spoke parables for understanding. He wasn't random but purposeful. He spoke truth because He is truth. I believe it's very simple. It's not complicated. Jesus says, *"Ask, and you will receive"* (John 16:24). He is ever-present.

In the end, I believe the Lord simplified things for Pearl. After her conversation with the Three, it wasn't complicated anymore. His love is forever!

# THIRTEEN

## Back at Home

The day of Pearl's funeral, I flew back home. That night, I drove over to a pharmacy to pick up some items. When I placed my items in the car, I sank into the driver's seat and cried. I was so exhausted. Somehow I had lost a bag on the way home containing Pearl's papers and items and the grief of it overwhelmed me. Even her body had been sent to the wrong funeral home, delaying the service.

There was only one other car in the parking lot. It started up and the female driver slowly manoeuvred up next to me. As she passed, I noticed her huge smile. I looked out my rear-view mirror as she drove away and couldn't believe my eyes. She had a huge sign in her back window that read "Wedding cake on board."

I was in awe. Suddenly, the Lord brought back the memory of Pearl in awe of the marriage supper of the Lamb. Was this a sign that I would meet her there?

Seeing is believing, they say. I have seen many signs along the way that go beyond our understanding. But the journey is fun! I'm so happy to be part of the mysteries which compound the many questions I already have. I know God has shown Pearl His love and I know He has shown me His love. It's beautiful.

> Again, the kingdom of heaven is like a merchant seeking beautiful pearls, who, when he had found one pearl of great price, went and sold all that he had and bought it. (Matthew 13:45–46)

That night, I awoke from a dream in which a tiny bird fell out of its nest. I saw God's hand reach down, cradle it in the palm of His hand, and say, "This is Pearl. She fell out of the nest, but I rescued her."

In the stillness of that moment, I felt incredible peace. That's when I realized how often we all fall out of the nest.

I believe this was a revelation from God for such a time as this, reminding me of His wondrous works even behind the scenes. This revelation was so profound to me!

Three days after Pearl passed on, the Lord led me to this verse which I wrote in my journal:

Yet I will rejoice in the Lord, I will joy in the
God of my salvation. (Habakkuk 3:18)

Pearl's favourite hymns were "In the Garden" and "The
Old Rugged Cross." At her funeral, my granddaughter sang
these songs.

A fellow named Gary, who serves on our church worship
team, every so often sings these same hymns in dedication to
Pearl and her memory. He never met Pearl, but her story has
touched many in her lifetime. She was loved by all.

As I close this book, I want to emphasize again the unique-
ness of God's love for us. His love is infinite and cannot be
measured. He is the Alpha and the Omega. He is the micro
and the macro in our lives, surrounding us all the time.

> And He said to me, "It is done! I am the
> Alpha and the Omega, the Beginning and
> the End. I will give of the fountain of the
> water of life freely to him who thirsts." (Rev-
> elation 21:6)

> Are not two sparrows sold for a copper coin?
> And not one of them falls to the ground
> apart from your Father's will. But the very
> hairs of your head are all numbered. Do not
> fear therefore; you are of more value than
> many sparrows. (Matthew 10:29–31)

My prayer is that everyone who reads this will seek Him. Every day is a new day. Everyone has their own story unique to you. God made us that way. God bless you!

> Now to the King eternal, immortal, invisible, to God who alone is wise, be honor and glory forever and ever. Amen. (1 Timothy 1:17)

# Acknowledgements

As it has been said before, Pearl was the life of any party. Her biggest party was her 100th Birthday Tea dubbed 'Pearl's Birthday Bash!' held at the retirement home. A special acknowledgement to Jill, my daughter, for all her help with organizing this event. As well, as the family who flew down from Calgary to attend and so many relatives and friends who were a part of Pearl's big event.

I designed a 'keepsake invitation' for her and mailed them out to her birthday list featuring a special picture of Pearl with her three great great grandkids at the time, titled 'Forever Young'. On the back of the card was a sample greeting for everyone to give to Pearl as they entered the party room. "You're still a young chick with a kick". The party was centered on 'Everything about Pearl' from framed memories on display to quizzes about Pearl and prizes! She had so much fun, a very special moment in time.

A special acknowledgement to Roy and Kathy Little (Roy would be Pearl's first cousin once removed). On their travels, they would drop in to visit with Pearl and attend many of Pearl's birthdays. Also, to all her many friends and relatives who kept in touch with Pearl throughout her years, whether by phone or in person, even by card or letter (she kept them all). She always felt blessed by all.

On Pearl's 101st birthday, my daughter and I had a small, intimate birthday party in a room at the nursing home. Pearl passed on five months later.

A special acknowledgement to Gary who serves on our church worship team. Every so often, he dedicates 'In the Garden' and 'The Old Rugged Cross' to Pearl. These were Pearl's favourites. He never met Pearl but her story has touched many in her lifetime. Everyone loved her.

A special acknowledgement to Carolyn Sandstrom for her creative photography, artistry and restoration of old photos. From the front cover, incorporating the colors of the era 1930 to the back cover featuring Pearl's pearls.

# About the Author

Janis Burnie Desjardins was born in Winnipeg, Manitoba, and lived within easy walking distance of two favourite places: her grandmother Pearl's home and Assiniboine Park. After finishing elementary school, Janis's family moved to Saskatoon, Saskatchewan, due to her father's work transfer. While she missed her friends in Winnipeg, making new ones was difficult with moving into rentals in different areas and different schools. Janis felt like a fish out of water.

In high school, the family finally settled down, and a friend invited her to church. It was there that she found new friends and solace in God. The hymn "It Is Well with My Soul" moved her deeply, bringing a newfound peace to her heart and inspiring her to write.

An English teacher recognized her talent for poetry and encouraged her to keep writing. Inspired by this support, Janis set a personal challenge to complete a 100-page book by the end of the year. She achieved this goal, finishing the final page just before midnight on New Year's Eve.

After high school, Janis spent a year at Business College, worked for a year at the University of Saskatchewan, and got married. Her husband secured a job in Calgary and a short time later, Janis did as well. Eventually she landed employment with the City of Calgary. They welcomed their baby daughter within a couple of years and during her maternity leave, Janis pursued writing again.

A friend invited her to attend a writing course at the Alexandra Writers' Centre with J. Michael Fay. There, she added short stories to her repertoire and participated in open readings of her work. Her poetry was published in *Blue Buffalo*, a publication of *The Dandelion Magazine Society* in Alberta.

Then several years later, her marriage ended, and Janis faced the challenges of being a single working mom. While pursuing her education. She worked full-time and attended courses at the University of Calgary, where she earned her Business Management Diploma. Janis credits this achievement to God and His unwavering love during difficult times, believing that all one has to do is receive what He has for each one of us.

Janis returned to writing and expanded her artistic pursuits to include jewellery making, silversmithing, oil painting, photo art, and greeting card design. Her work has been featured in the *Calgary Herald* and sold in shops in Calgary and Bragg Creek. Now remarried, she and her husband are enjoying their retirement years.

Several years ago, their pastor at that time invited Janis to contribute to the church's weekly bulletin. She would wait for the Lord's prompt, which sometimes came just the night before Sunday. She wrote and printed the bulletin, thus, she was in a position to do that. The Lord was teaching her to 'wait on Him' and His work plan for everyone is certainly worth waiting for. The Lord was teaching patience and trust, and reinforced that He never fails. After this, she wrote online for Partners in Christ Ministries in Ontario.

On October 28, 2020, the Lord inspired Janis with this declaration: "Father God - You move above all the noise."